E*conomy Update: 2009*

Stephen L. Slavin

Union County College
Cranford, New Jersey

The New School University
New York City

McGraw-Hill Irwin

Boston   Burr Ridge, IL   Dubuque, IA   New York   San Francisco   St. Louis
Bangkok   Bogotá   Caracas   Kuala Lumpur   Lisbon   London   Madrid   Mexico City
Milan   Montreal   New Delhi   Santiago   Seoul   Singapore   Sydney   Taipei   Toronto

McGraw-Hill
Irwin

ECONOMY UPDATE: 2009

Published by McGraw-Hill/Irwin, a business unit of The McGraw-Hill Companies, Inc., 1221 Avenue of the Americas, New York, NY, 10020. Copyright © 2009, 2008, 2005, 2002, 1999, 1996, 1994, 1991, 1989 by The McGraw-Hill Companies, Inc. All rights reserved. No part of this publication may be reproduced or distributed in any form or by any means, or stored in a database or retrieval system, without the prior written consent of The McGraw-Hill Companies, Inc., including, but not limited to, in any network or other electronic storage or transmission, or broadcast for distance learning.

Some ancillaries, including electronic and print components, may not be available to customers outside the United States.

This book is printed on acid-free paper.

1 2 3 4 5 6 7 8 9 0 QPD/QPD 0 9

ISBN 978-0-07-734486-3
MHID 0-07-734486-3

www.mhhe.com

The Great Recession

The economic fundamentals are strong.
—John McCain, September 15, 2008

Our economy is fundamentally sound.
—Herbert Hoover, 1931

2008 was not a good year for the American economy. A recession, which began in December 2007, grew progressively worse. Our entire financial system was unraveling, and employment fell each month. By year's end the U.S. Treasury and the Federal Reserve had committed over $2 trillion to rescue ailing banks, insurance companies, and other large corporations. And despite this huge financial commitment, economic conditions were getting still worse in early 2009.

Because of the interconnectedness of the world's financial system, our financial crisis quickly spread. Of the trillions of dollars in losses suffered by American financial institutions, a sizable chunk was lost by foreign investors. By early 2009 the United Kingdom, Germany, France, and Italy had already put in place their own bailout programs, and several other nations would soon follow suit. By now there was a worldwide recession. But look at the bright side: All this terrible news has made your economics course a lot more relevant.

Are We Going Into Another Great Depression?

When President Hoover proclaimed our economy "fundamentally sound," we were in the depths of the Great Depression. While the economy was in free fall, the federal government did very little to arrest the decline. The big question on everyone's mind in early 2009 was this: Will the current recession turn into another Great Depression?

The answer was "no." We learned enough, especially in the 1930s and the early 1940s to prevent another depression from ever happening again. The most powerful measure the federal government can take is to spend huge amounts of money to compensate for any shortfalls in private sector spending. Large tax cuts and government loans will also stimulate the economy. Nearly all the stimulus supplied in 2008 was in the form of tax rebates and government loans, many of which will never be paid back. By the end of 2009, however, the federal government will have spent hundreds of billions of dollars and provided hundreds of billions more in tax cuts to shore up our economy.

If we were not in another Great Depression, what should we call the latest economic downturn? Some people have been calling it a mini-depression, and others, "the Great Recession."[1] The two worst recessions we have had since the Great Depression itself were in 1973–75 and in 1981–82. Both lasted 16 months. According to the National

---

[1]Perhaps the first person to call this "the Great Recession" was Diana Furchtgott-Roth, a former chief economist at the U.S. Department of Labor, in an article, "The Great Recession of 2008?" in *The American*, December 21, 2007, www.american.com/archive/2007/december-12-07/the-great-recession-of-2008.

Bureau of Economic Research, the current recession began in December 2007: In April 2009 it became the longest economic downturn on record since the early 1930s. But in the spring of 2009, it was still not yet certain if this recession would be worse than those of 1973–75 and 1981–82.[2]

Anatomy of a Recession

When economists try to figure out if we are in a recession, what data do they look at? Three closely watched indicators are Real GDP growth, the unemployment rate, and the monthly change in employment. If Real GDP declines and if the unemployment rate is rising, these are two strong indications that we may be in a recession. And if employment falls substantially for several months, it would be very likely that a recession has already begun. Now let's look at the record since the beginning of 2007.

Real GDP Growth   Real GDP measures our nation's output of goods and services for one year at constant prices. When Real GDP declines for two consecutive quarters, then surely our economy is in a recession. If that decline is substantial—say at an annual rate of more than 3 percent—then we know that the recession is quite severe.

Figure 1 shows Real GDP growth from the first quarter of 2007 through the first quarter of 2009. In the fourth quarter of 2007 Real GDP declined slightly, and then rose

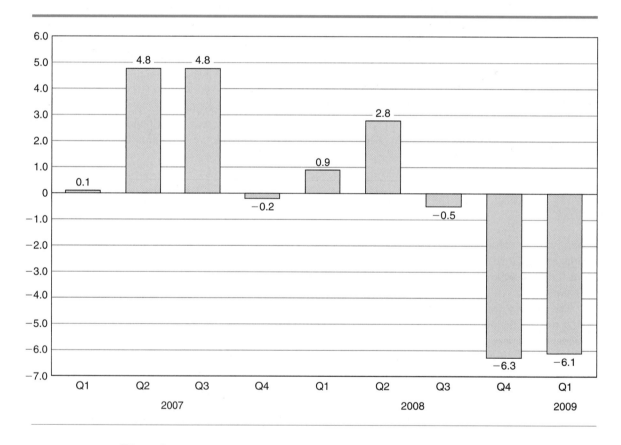

Figure 1

Annual GDP Growth, Percentage Change from Previous Quarter, 2007–2009
The annual growth rate of 6.1 percent for the first quarter of 2009 is an "advance figure," which will be subject to two revisions—one in late May and the final one in late June.
Source: Bureau of Economic Analysis (www.bea.gov).

---

[2]Turn to page 12 of this book, where you'll find a box providing capsule summaries of all our post–World War II recessions.

Percentage Changes in Real GDP*

One of the most important equations in economics is $GDP = C + I + G + X_n$, which you can find on page 176 of *Economics* and *Macroeconomics*. C is consumption, I is investment, G is government expenditures, and X_n is net exports (i.e., exports − imports). *GDP is the nation's expenditure on all the final goods and services produced during the year at market prices.* Real GDP does not reflect changes in the price level, so it allows us to make comparisons of output among different time periods.

In Figure 1 we saw the percentage changes in Real GDP from the first quarter of 2007 through the first quarter of 2009. Table A gives us a chance to see the percentage changes in the components of Real GDP during this period and helps us understand why Real GDP rose and fell during this period.

Please keep in mind that because the components of GDP shown in Table A have different weights, the percentage changes for C, I, G, and X_n don't add up to the percentage change for Real GDP in each quarter. C, for example, accounts for about 70 percent of GDP.

Why then did Real GDP show such slow growth since the fourth quarter of 2007, with declines in the fourth quarter of 2007 and from the third quarter of 2008 through the first quarter of 2009? The most important contributors were declining I and slow growth of C through the second quarter of 2008, and then declining C since the third quarter of that year.

Investment falls during every recession, but its fall since the fourth quarter of 2007 was more pronounced than in nearly all post–World War II recessions. This was mainly because of the rapid decline in residential housing investment.

But what is especially unusual about the Great Recession is the decline in the level of C in the third and fourth quarters of 2008. We would need to go back to the Great Depression to find two consecutive quarters when Real C actually declined.

Why has consumption fallen so much during this recession? There are two main explanations. First, there has been a very rapid decline in employment, as nearly 6 million people have lost their jobs between the beginning of the recession in December 2007 and April 2009. These workers and their families have been forced to cut back sharply on their consumption. In addition, many others have very substantially increased their saving because they are afraid they may soon lose their jobs.

You'll notice that G increased steadily through 2008, helping to offset declines in C and I. And finally, X_n fell for all but one quarter. Until 2007 we had been running huge trade deficits. Because the worldwide recession begun in the United States took almost a year to spread throughout most of the world, our imports began falling well before our exports. Consequently, X_n fell sharply since the beginning of the recession. Because the trade deficit pushes down GDP growth, the declining deficit is reflected in Table A by a positive percentage growth in X_n.

TABLE A	Percent Change in Components of Real GDP, First Quarter of 2007–First Quarter of 2009, at Annual Rates*				
	C	I	G	X_n**	Real GDP
2007 I	3.9	−9.6	0.9	−5.9	0.1
II	2.0	6.2	3.9	8.3	4.8
III	2.0	3.5	3.8	11.6	4.8
IV	1.0	−11.9	0.8	5.6	−0.2
2008 I	0.9	−5.8	1.9	4.9	0.9
II	1.2	−11.5	3.9	21.2	2.8
III	−3.8	0.4	5.8	8.0	−0.5
IV	−4.3	−23.0	1.3	−3.2	−6.3
2009 I	2.2	−51.8	−3.9	—	−6.1

*Because the components of Real GDP have different weights, the percentage changes for C, I, G, and X_n don't add up to the percentage change for Real GDP in each quarter.

**Net exports have been negative since the early 1970s. But since the fourth quarter of 2005 net exports have been decreasing. In this table, the percentage that this negative number has been decreasing is shown as a positive number. Similarly, in the two instances in which net exports have increased—the first quarter of 2007 and the fourth quarter of 2008—the percentage change is shown as a negative number. The main point is that shrinking net exports increase GDP, while rising net exports decrease GDP.

Source: Table 1.1.1, Real Gross Domestic Product and Related Measures: Percent Change From Preceding Period, www.bea.gov.

in the first and second quarters of 2008. But then it fell in the third and fourth quarters. When Real GDP fell at an annual rate of 6.3 percent in the October–December quarter of 2008, it was quite clear that we were in a very severe recession. The accompanying box provides a more detailed look at Real GDP growth since the beginning of 2007.

Real GDP continued to fall very substantially in the first quarter of 2009 and was expected to continue falling in the second quarter. Two important questions were: would it also fall in the third and fourth quarters?

Figure 2

Monthly Unemployment Rate,
2007–2009
Source: U.S. Bureau of Labor Statistics.

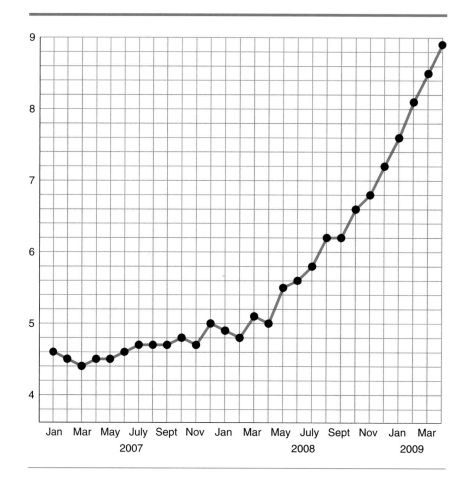

The Unemployment Rate   The unemployment rate is another important measure of our economic performance, and it always rises substantially during recessions. Often, however, it doesn't rise appreciably until well after a recession has begun, and, interestingly, it seldom peaks until a few months after it has ended. By glancing at the unemployment rate shown in Figure 2, we can see that it stayed below 5 percent for nearly all of 2007 as well as for the first two months of 2008. Not until August did it top 6 percent. By comparison, at the end of the 1981–82 recession our unemployment rate was in double digits, and at the end of the 1973–75 recession it reached almost 9 percent. In April 2009, our unemployment rate rose to 8.9 percent and was expected to go still higher.

Monthly Change in Employment   Perhaps the best indicator of the severity of the Great Recession is the monthly change in employment shown in Figure 3. Employment rose each month in 2007, and then fell each month in 2008. You'll notice that monthly employment fell by an average of well over 600,000 beginning in November 2008.

   Our employment situation was even worse than it appeared to be in Figure 3. Every year about 1.8 million workers enter or re-enter our labor force. To prevent rising unemployment, our economy needs to generate 1,800,000 jobs over the course of a year. But in 2007 we added just 1 million jobs. So we were 800,000 short of the number we needed to keep unemployment from rising.

   The employment story for 2008 was considerably worse. Employment fell each month, with declines accelerating since September. Looking at the entire year, we needed to add 1,800,000 jobs, but we actually lost a total of just under 3 million jobs.

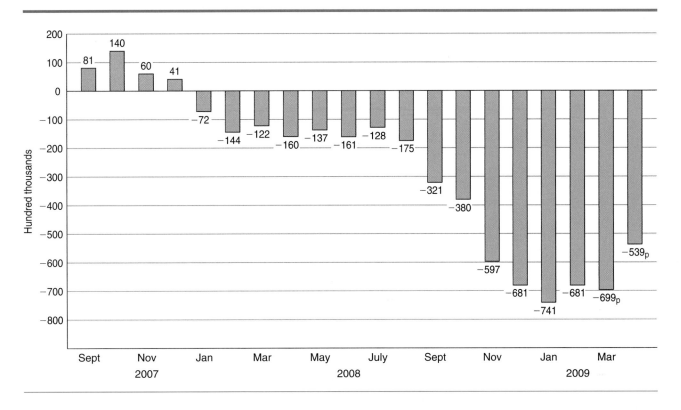

Figure 3

Employment in Total Nonfarm Sector: Over-the-Month Change, 2007–2009
p = preliminary data
Source: U.S. Bureau of Labor Statistics.

As we see in Figure 3, according to preliminary data, employment in April 2009 fell by 539,000, after declines in February of 681,000 and in March of 699,000. Did this signal that the worst was over and that the Great Recession was finally coming to an end? While the loss of over half a million jobs was hardly good news—especially if yours was one of the jobs that was lost—it was 200,000 less than January's employment decline.

The Causes of the Great Recession

What caused the Great Recession? The bursting of the housing bubble set off the subprime mortgage crisis and the subsequent financial meltdown. Sharply rising oil prices—if you'll forgive the pun—threw still more oil on the fire. Let's consider each of these causes, in turn.

The Bursting of the Housing Bubble

After rising at a rate of slightly less than 3 percent a year during the 1990s, home prices jumped nationally by an average of nearly 9 percent per year from 2000 to mid-2006. But in the summer of 2006, the bubble finally burst. By April 2009, home prices fell by more than 30 percent. This reversal had an adverse affect on the economy, leading to a financial crisis and, ultimately, to the Great Recession.

Tens of millions of Americans had been borrowing heavily on their homes to meet their everyday expenses. When housing prices began to fall, home equity loans became increasingly difficult to obtain. Hundreds of thousands of workers in construction and real estate were thrown out of work. Still, had the damages been limited to this economic sector, we would not have gone into a recession.

The Subprime Mortgage Crisis and Financial Meltdown

A high proportion of the homes in foreclosure were owned by families that held subprime mortgages. And it was the subprime mortgage crisis, which, in turn, set off the financial meltdown. Mortgage brokers had steered millions of relatively low-income families into buying homes they could not afford. As hundreds of thousands of people began to default on their mortgages, banks, hedge funds, brokerage houses, and other mortgage lenders were staggered by huge losses. To make matters still worse, the bulk of these mortgages had been sliced and diced into exotic securities known as *collateralized debt obligations*. The big problem with *CDOs* was that no one knew how much they were actually worth. They could not be sold, if at all, for more than a fraction of their face value. Financial institutions, some of which had paid tens of billions of dollars for these securities, were stuck with them.

CDOs are collections of loans that are bundled together, usually by an investment bank or by a brokerage house, and sold to investors. The loans can range from short-term corporate debt to 30-year home mortgages. These loans are held as collateral by the owners of the CDOs, who then receive a steady stream of income.

Suppose your bank was holding $10 billion in CDOs, $1 billion in cash, and had $8 billion in deposits. It therefore had assets of $11 billion and liabilities of $8 billion. But it could not sell those CDOs without taking a huge loss. In other words, those CDOs were worth a lot less than $10 billion. What the bank really needed to do was to estimate how much it could sell them for, and write down its total assets. If it estimated that the CDOs could be sold for just $5 billion, then the bank would have total assets of just $6 billion and liabilities of $8 billion. It would, in effect, be bankrupt.

Obviously the U.S. government did not want to see hundreds upon hundreds of banks going bankrupt. In the long run—say over the course of two or three years—it would be necessary to rid the banks of these "toxic assets." But there was a much more pressing problem, which was to provide our entire financial system with enough money to enable it to avoid a financial meltdown.

Although the Federal Reserve, and subsequently, the U.S. Treasury, made a valiant, if belated effort to provide these institutions with liquidity, the financial meltdown was in full swing by early 2008. The main effect on the economy was that the financial markets were seizing up, making it very difficult to obtain loans. A secondary effect was that the banks and other financial institutions were laying off hundreds of thousands of employees.[3]

It may be years before we can figure out why our financial system so quickly unraveled, and how such venerable institutions as Citigroup, Bank of America, Merrill Lynch, A.I.G., Morgan Stanley, Lehman Brothers, and even government-backed Fannie Mae and Freddie Mac managed to make such poor financial decisions. Left to their own devices, the titans of the financial services industries were sorely tempted by the opportunity to make huge profits, even though this required taking huge risks as well. Just 8 percent of our labor force was employed in financial services, but that sector accounted for nearly 30 percent of all corporate profits during the last few years.

The prevalent view, especially among Democratic politicians, is that the deregulation of our financial institutions in recent years has been largely responsible for the financial crisis. But *Time* magazine financial writer, Justin Fox, has a somewhat different take on deregulation. He has noted that the new unregulated financial institutions that have sprung

---

[3]The housing bubble, the subprime mortgage mess, and the financial crisis are discussed on pages 353–55 of *Economics* and *Macroeconomics*.

up over the last four decades have taken over much of the mortgage business once monopolized by banks.

> Lawmakers and regulators responded in the 1990s not by setting parameters for these new players—investment banks, hedge funds, private equity funds, etc.—but by giving bank holding companies more freedom to enter under-regulated lines of business.[4]

Interestingly, in late March 2009, Treasury Secretary Timothy Geithner began negotiations with Congress in the hopes of being granted regulatory authority over these financial institutions—a great example of closing the barn door more than a decade after the horses got loose.

Rising Oil Prices

One other major factor played a role in bringing on the Great Recession—the spectacular run-up of worldwide oil prices. In 2007 the price of oil jumped 57 percent to $96 a barrel, and by July 2008 it set a record of $147. Gasoline was over $4 a gallon. People were cutting back on driving, and automobile sales were falling rapidly. By the end of the year, General Motors, Ford, and Chrysler were on the verge of bankruptcy.

Perhaps the only *good* economic news was the rapid decline in the price of oil, which fell below $35 a barrel in January 2009. This came in response to the worldwide recession, which depressed the demand for oil, and also dampened the ardor of oil speculators. By then gasoline was under $2 a gallon. But these price declines, however welcome, came much too late to stop economic conditions from deteriorating even further.

Restoring a Normally Functioning Financial System

In the fall of 2008 our economy was beset by two increasingly severe economic problems—a financial meltdown and what was looking more and more like a long and deep recession. These problems called for a two-pronged attack—getting our financial institutions functioning normally again and preventing the recession from getting much worse. The administration of George W. Bush made a start on the first problem, leaving it to the incoming administration of Barack Obama to do the bulk of the work, as well as to deal with the second.

The $700,000,000,000 Bailout   With our financial institutions holding trillions of dollars in collateralized debt obligations as well as in other securities of dubious value, they had no choice but to write down the value of what were now termed "toxic assets." Because of the intertwined ownership of many of these securities, it was unclear who owed what to whom. There was a great danger that a large part of our financial sector would soon be toppled like falling dominos, possibly setting off a worldwide financial meltdown. So in late September 2008, in the heat of the national election campaign, enormous pressure was brought to bear on Congress to do something big—and to do it fast.

After two weeks of political maneuvering, on October 3, 2008, Congress passed, and President George W. Bush signed into law, the $700 billion Troubled Assets Relief Program. This gave the Treasury the power to purchase illiquid assets from banks and other financial institutions and even to buy their stock. Treasury officials were hoping that the trading of these assets would eventually resume.

---

[4]Justin Fox, "The Financial Crisis Blame Game," *Time,* December 30, 2008. http://www.time.com/time/specials/packages/0,28757,1869041,00.html

Much of the impetus for the passage of the bailout was built around a plea for compassion for the millions of homeowners facing foreclosure. Included in the wording of the law was a requirement that the Treasury "develop a plan that seeks to maximize assistance for homeowners." But the legislation allowed the Treasury to spend the first $350 billion almost entirely at its own discretion. In what some considered a "bait and switch" scheme, Treasury officials were soon saying that funding to forestall home foreclosures would not be productive; the TARP funds would be better spent buying up troubled banks and helping healthy banks buy failing banks and other financial institutions. The hope was that this in-flow of cash would get banks to start lending again.

But most bankers receiving these funds were reluctant to lend them out, afraid that if economic conditions continued to deteriorate, these new loans would go bad. In the spring of 2009 they were still holding most of these funds, and, in the case of Citigroup and several other troubled banks, were using this money to defray their losses. Mostly, the first $350 billion of the bailout was used as an insurance policy against the possibility of a prolonged recession.

In January 2009, at the behest of President Bush and President-elect Obama, Congress voted to release the second $350 billion of the bailout funds to the Treasury. But many financial experts believed it would take at least another trillion dollars in bailout money to get our financial system functioning efficiently.

By the end of 2008, in addition to the $700 billion bailout, the Federal Reserve and the Treasury had incurred at least another $8 trillion in direct and indirect financial obligations. For example, the Treasury guaranteed payment for more than $300 billion of Citigroup's liabilities. And the Federal Reserve had issued over $1.7 trillion in emergency loans to troubled corporations and financial institutions.

Stopping Mortgage Foreclosures   By early 2009 1 out of 11 homes was in foreclosure. During this process, which on average takes about 18 months, the homeowner typically makes no mortgage payments and no repairs. In addition, abandoned homes are often stripped and vandalized. Mortgage lenders lose about half the outstanding loan amount. As more than 2 million foreclosed homes are put back on the market each year, they continue to drive down housing prices.

On February 18, 2009, President Obama announced a $275 billion plan to help as many as 9 million American homeowners refinance their mortgages or avert foreclosure. The plan, which went into effect on March 4, had three main parts:

1. Assist some 4 million families who were at risk of losing their homes by providing incentives to lenders who altered loan terms to make them more affordable.

2. Help about 5 million homeowners who were current in their payments, but did not have enough equity in their homes to be able to refinance their mortgages to take advantage of lower interest rates.

3. Provide Fannie Mae and Freddie Mac with $200 billion of additional financing to help shore up their mortgages.

While this plan will help millions of families keep their homes, it does nothing to help even more families whose homes are "under water"—that is, their mortgage debt is considerably more than the market value of their homes. Why keep sinking even more money into your home if you're not building up equity? Why pay, say $2,000 a month in mortgage payments, heating, and real estate taxes, when you could rent a comparable home or apartment for half as much?

By the end of March 2009, more than one out of every five homeowners owed more on their mortgages than their homes were worth. Declining home prices left them with negative equity—i.e. their homes were under water.

Every month, hundreds of thousands of these homeowners have simply been walking away from their homes. Given a monetary incentive—namely a substantial reduction in their mortgage debt—most of these families would have a much greater incentive to remain in their homes and continue making their mortgage payments. Still, by helping millions of homeowners avoid foreclosure, the Obama plan may finally stem the decline in the prices of homes. That, in turn, would provide welcome relief to those whose homes were under water.

The Obama Bank Rescue Plan   On March 23, 2009, Treasury Secretary Timothy Geithner rolled out the last major initiative to restore a normally functioning financial system. It entailed buying up to $1 trillion in bank-owned real estate assets using funds that are almost entirely supplied by the Federal Reserve and the Treasury. Private investors would receive as much as 92 cents of low-cost government loans and loan guarantees for every dollar they invested.

The Federal Deposit Insurance Corporation would set up auctions for banks to sell bundles of mortgages to the highest bidders. In addition, the Treasury would help finance public-private investment funds to buy up unmarketable CDOs.

But the plan appeared to have three serious drawbacks. Potential purchasers of bank-held mortgages—hedge funds, private equity funds, pension funds, insurance companies, and even some banks—had been offering just 30 cents on the dollar, even if most of the borrowers were still current in their payments. But the banks, not wanting to write off such huge losses, were refusing to accept less than 60 cents on the dollar. Until the FDIC actually sets up the auctions, it will be hard to know how quickly the banks will sell off their toxic assets.

Another drawback of the plan is that even the infusion of $1 trillion may not be enough to restore many of the larger banks to financial health. What if, after the sale of their toxic assets, some banks find that their liabilities exceed their assets? In that case these banks would be bankrupt, and would need to be taken over by healthy banks or by the FDIC.

A final drawback is that private investors, who may possibly make large profits, are risking relatively small sums of money. But the government, which is risking much greater sums, may end up losing hundreds of billions of dollars if the formerly toxic assets decline in value. So the bank rescue plan, from the viewpoint of the private investor vis-à-vis the government, can be summed up as "Heads, I win; tails, you lose." (See box on page 10.)

Given all these potential difficulties, one may ask why we are proceeding with this plan. If it does succeed, then its shortcomings can be overlooked. Furthermore, consider one alternative—doing nothing. As Fed Chairman Ben Bernanke observed, "Until we stabilize the financial system, a sustainable economic recovery will remain out of reach."[5]

An ongoing worry was whether any of the nation's largest financial institutions would fail if the recession got much worse. So the Federal Reserve and the U.S. Treasury designed a stress test to determine which of the largest 19 financial institutions—those with assets of over $100 billion—were most vulnerable (see the box on page 10). The good news was that none was in danger of bankruptcy in the foreseeable future. The bad news was that 10 of these institutions needed a capital infusion totaling $75 billion.

Fighting the Great Recession

The federal government has two basic policy weapons for fighting recessions—fiscal policy and monetary policy. Fiscal policy, which involves government spending and taxes, is conducted by the president and Congress. Monetary policy, which is largely controlling the rate of growth of the money supply, is the responsibility of the Federal Reserve.

---

[5]David Von Drehle and Michael Scherer, "Obama's Reform Agenda: Is He Trying to Do Too Much?" *Time,* March 13, 2009, www.time.com/time/politics/article/0,8599,1884630,00.html.

The Financial Institution Stress Test

Federal Reserve and U.S. Treasury officials were concerned that some of the nation's largest financial institutions might go bankrupt if the recession worsened. So the Federal Reserve and the U.S. Treasury designed a stress test to determine which of the 19 largest banks—those with assets of over $100 billion—were most vulnerable. They spent most of February through April of 2009 examining mortgage loan, consumer loan, and other loan portfolios. A major purpose of these tests was to instill confidence in our financial system by ensuring that it could weather a prolonged recession. The good news was that none of the banks was in danger of bankruptcy in the foreseeable future. The bad news was that some of these institutions needed a capital infusion.

The results, announced on May 7, indicated that 10 of the 19 banks examined needed to raise a total of $75 billion in new capital. The four largest are listed in Table B. As you'll notice, Bank of America needs to raise nearly $35 billion, close to half the total needed by the 10 financial institutions. Of the four companies listed, three are traditional banks, and the fourth, GMAC (General Motors Acceptance Corporation) which provides

TABLE B

Banks Needing to Raise Capital
May 7, 2009
(in billions of dollars)

Bank of America	$33.9
Wells Fargo	13.7
GMAC	11.5
Citigroup	5.5

Source: http://www.usatoday.com/money/industries/banking/2009-05-07-bank-stress-tests_N.htm.

car loans, was recently converted into a bank by the Federal Reserve.

How will these companies raise the needed capital? Essentially three ways—sell off assets, issue new shares of common stock, and convert some of their preferred stock into common stock. Much of the money from the Treasury's $700 billion bailout was used to purchase preferred stock of banks, so the U.S. government may end up owning substantial blocs of the banks' common stock.

For most of 2008, we depended almost entirely on monetary policy to try to head off the recession that had begun in December 2007. Aside from a $168 billion stimulus package consisting mainly of taxpayer rebates that was passed in early 2008, there were no fiscal policy measures taken during that year. Instead we counted on the Federal Reserve to ease credit, which it did for the entire year. By year's end, it had reduced some short-term interest rates to close to zero.

What did the Fed have to show for those efforts? Two large economic sectors are especially responsive to falling interest rates—housing and car buying. As you well know, housing prices fell through the entire year while housing sales declined sharply. And the auto industry had its worst sales year since 1992 with General Motors and Chrysler pushed to the brink of bankruptcy. At best, monetary policy prevented a bad recession from growing still worse. By late 2008 it was quite clear that the ball was now in the court of the fiscal policy-makers. Comparisons were being made with conditions during the Great Depression, and people were looking for drastic solutions. It was time to call the doctor—Dr. John Maynard Keynes.

Keynesian Economics

John Maynard Keynes, arguably the greatest economist of the 20th century, is the godfather of fiscal policy, which calls for running large budget deficits to fight recessions. The problem during recessions is insufficient aggregate demand—the sum of consumption spending, investment spending, government spending, and net exports. By late 2008 consumption spending and investment spending had fallen substantially. If aggregate demand is falling, said Keynes, then we need to push it back up. And the way to do that is to drastically increase government spending.

What kind of government spending programs did Keynes support? Any that would put people to work, even if it meant hiring some of them to dig holes and others to fill them up again. Of course Keynes preferred jobs that would produce useful goods and services, but the most important thing was to put the unemployed back to work. They would then spend their paychecks, thereby boosting consumption—the main component of aggregate demand.

To a large degree, Keynes provided the employment policy blueprint to get us out of the Great Depression. President Franklin Roosevelt's New Deal quickly put millions of Americans back to work by creating government jobs for them. The basic idea was to put money into people's pockets, which they would then spend. Their spending would stimulate business, and as sales rose, employers would hire more workers. This process, which was called *pump priming*—since it got money flowing through the economy the way water would flow through a pipe—worked as advertised, and economic activity picked up sharply.

Roosevelt's New Deal program was initially a great success. But then, in 1937, the president, in a misguided effort to balance the federal budget well before the depression was over, was largely responsible for causing the very sharp 1937–38 business downturn. The Federal Reserve made matters still worse by tightening credit. It was only the subsequent massive spending on armaments leading up to our involvement in World War II that finally pulled us out of the Great Depression.[6]

President Obama has talked about creating or preserving up to 4 million jobs. He and his economic advisors, along with most members of Congress, have embraced the Keynesian policy prescription of boosting aggregate demand. Well aware of the shortcomings of Roosevelt's New Deal spending program, they agree on the importance of spending enough money for as long as needed.[7]

The 2009 Stimulus Package: An Imperfect Means to a Necessary End

Like so many other controversial laws, the 2009 economic stimulus package reflected a compromise among Senate Republicans, Senate Democrats, and President Barack Obama. In the end, this needed measure was far from perfect.

The Politics of Cutting Taxes and Raising Government Spending
What kind of economic stimulus package did the Democrats want, and what kind of stimulus package did the Republicans want? Both agreed that there should be large increases in government spending and large tax cuts. The big disagreement between them was by *how much* spending should be increased and by *how much* taxes should be cut. The Republicans wanted much—or even all—of the stimulus package devoted to tax cuts, while the Democrats strongly favored more spending. In January 2009, as a newly elected president and Congress took office, it was clear that spending increases would be greater than tax cuts. The big question was, By how *much* would spending increases exceed tax cuts?

Although the Democrats held large majorities in both houses of Congress, some compromise with the Republicans was necessary in the Senate. A bill supported by over half the voting Senators passes—but individual senators may filibuster a bill they don't like, preventing the Senate from holding a vote. To close debate (and end a filibuster), the majority party needs 60 votes. The Democrats, with the support of two independent senators, still needed the support of at least two Republican senators to bring Senate bills to a vote.

Senators Olympia Snowe and Susan Collins of Maine and Senator Arlen Specter[8] of Pennsylvania provided the needed Republican votes to pass the economic stimulus bill,

---

[6]To read further about the Great Depression and the New Deal, see pages 7–10 of this book.

[7]To read more about Keynesian economics in *Economics* or in *Macroeconomics*, see pages 261–70; 368–69.

[8]About 10 weeks later Senator Specter announced that he was leaving the Republican party to join the Democratic party. This gave the Democrats 59 votes, and, if Al Franken is finally certified as the winner in the extremely close Minnesota senatorial election of 2008, they would have a filibuster-proof majority of 60 votes.

but only after the Democrats agreed to reduce spending programs by some $100 billion. President Obama signed the bill on February 17, 2009.

The Economic Stimulus Act of 2009   The $787 billion stimulus package included $287 billion in tax cuts and $500 billion in government spending. Here are its major items:

- $233 billion in tax cuts for individuals and families: Up to $400 tax credit for individuals in 2009 and 2010 (cost: $116 billion) and alternate minimum tax patch (cost: $70 billion)[9]

- $106 billion for education and job training: help for states to prevent cutbacks and layoffs, mostly in education (cost: $54 billion) and additional financing for special education and low-income children (cost: $25 billion)

- $87 billion to states in increased federal contribution to Medicaid costs

- $78 billion for jobless people: expand unemployment benefits (cost: $36 billion) and help for laid off workers to keep group health insurance (cost: $25 billion)[10]

- $48 billion for highway and bridge construction and mass transit

- $44 billion for energy, including modernizing the electric grid

- $41 billion for infrastructure, water, and the environment

- $29 billion for health, science, and research

- $21 billion for energy investments: expand incentives for renewable energy production facilities (cost: $14 billion)

- $20 billion to expand food stamp benefits

The Four Questions   During the congressional debate, four major questions were raised about the effects of such a large stimulus plan. Let's consider them next.

1. **Will the stimulus package end the recession?**   The most important macroeconomic policy lesson learned from the Great Depression is that after we opt to stimulate the economy with massive federal spending, we must be careful not to try to reduce the deficit too quickly. If we *do* spend enough, and not worry about balancing the federal budget, then we can expect the stimulus package to help end the Great Recession.

   If it has not ended by late 2009, it is very likely that another round of tax cuts and spending increases will be enacted. With elections coming up in 2010, no member of Congress will want to face the voters with our economy still mired in recession.

2. **Will most of the stimulus package be wasted on make-work jobs?**   Given the speed with which Congress has had to act, and taking into account the political realities, some of the jobs created are of a make-work nature. But quickly putting millions of people back to work, and giving them paychecks to spend, has a higher priority than taking the time to provide truly useful jobs for the unemployed. Still, the large majority of jobs newly created or saved—whether repairing highways and bridges, hiring more teachers, weatherizing federal buildings, or computerizing medical records—are clearly not make-work jobs.

---

[9]This tax was intended to collect income tax from very rich families who had been paying no taxes. But in recent years it was imposed on millions of upper-middle-class families. Each year Congress passed legislation that enabled these families to pay little or none of the alternative minimum tax. Since this "patch" is passed every year, it is misleading to count it as part of the economic stimulus package.

[10]The law increases unemployment benefits by $25 a week and allows states to extend those benefits through the end of 2009. It also provides jobless workers with an additional 20 weeks in unemployment benefits, and 13 weeks on top of that if they live in what's deemed a high unemployment state, of which there were more than 30 in the spring of 2009. Several governors, led by Mark Sanford of South Carolina, have refused to accept at least part of these funds because they believed that at the end of the year their states would then be obligated to continue paying the higher weekly benefits.

It is extremely important to get the unemployed on the payroll as quickly as possible. Projects which need to go through a bidding process and months of planning before many people are put work would not be nearly as effective in ending the recession as those that are "shovel ready."

3. **Will massive budget deficits ignite another round of inflation?** Given the seriousness of the recession, which has been accompanied by sharply falling housing prices, renewed inflation should certainly not be an immediate worry. In fact, many economists are worried about the prospects of deflation—*a broadly based decline in the price level, not for a month or two but for a period of years.*

Is there a danger of deflation right now? The Consumer Price Index, which rose by 4.1 percent in 2007, rose by just 0.1 percent in 2008, the lowest increase in 54 years. In the fourth quarter of that year, the CPI, driven by sharply declining energy prices, actually fell at an annual rate of 12.7 percent. But it seems likely that fears of falling prices in 2009 are overblown. By the time you read these words, you'll know whether or not they were.

Still, renewed inflation is a real possibility, given the amount of money that the Federal Reserve has been pumping into the economy since mid-2008, and also because of our huge federal budget deficits. Once economic recovery is in full swing, the Federal Reserve will need to stop increasing the money supply, while Congress, in conjunction with the Obama administration, will have to substantially reduce the deficit.

4. **Is the Deficit Too Big?** Even by the middle of fiscal year 2009, which began on October 1, 2008, it was not yet clear how large the deficit would be. But it was on track to set a post–World War II record as a percent of GDP. The previous record of 6 percent set in 1983 would be surpassed, so the only question was—by how much? In late March 2009, the Congressional Budget Office forecast a deficit of $1.85 trillion for fiscal year 2009—about 13 percent of GDP. This would be quadruple the record $459 billion deficit we ran in fiscal year 2008. Even though President Obama hopes we can cut the deficit by more than two-thirds by 2013, we may be running deficits of more than $1 trillion for the next few years.

The size of the deficit will almost certainly be a major issue in the 2010 Congressional election. Most Republican candidates will point to the huge deficits of fiscal years 2009 and 2010 and tell the voters that the Democrats are not only wasting hundreds of billions of taxpayer dollars, but are driving our nation into bankruptcy. But most Americans want the government to take whatever steps are needed to end the Great Recession. Still, we need to ask what will be the long run consequences of running such large deficits.

Is the deficit too big? In the long run deficits this big would drive our government into bankruptcy, because it could not continue borrowing such huge sums of money indefinitely. But we ran much larger deficits during wartime—most recently during the Second World War.

If you *still* believe that the deficit is too big, please consider the alternative. If we don't run humongous deficits at least through fiscal year 2010, we could be faced by a continuing recession, and the possibility that it could even turn into a full blown depression. As large the deficit has grown, if the Great Recession has not ended by late 2009, we may conclude that our mistake was not running an even larger deficit.

The Chinese Stimulus Plan

Rivaling the size of our economic stimulus plan, China, with an economy perhaps 15 or 20 percent of the size of ours, created a $586 billion fiscal stimulus program. It was launched in November 2008, and unlike the American plan, most of its funding was intended to expand the economy's infrastructure—mainly railways, airports, power plants, and highways. In addition, the government made it much easier for banks to extend business loans, which more than doubled between the spring of 2008 and the spring of 2009. Significantly, China has probably averted the worldwide recession, although its annual growth rate dipped from 10 percent to about 6 percent. Indeed, in the first quarter of 2009, China passed the United States in the sale of motor vehicles, becoming the world's largest market.

on the web

You can track our economy's performance on two Web sites. Go to www.bls.gov for monthly updates on the unemployment rate, employment, and the Consumer Price Index. Go to www.bea.gov for quarterly Real GDP data.

Conclusion

As you read these words, you will know whether or not the Great Recession was our most severe economic downturn since the Great Depression of the 1930s. You will also know how successful the government was in restoring normality to the operations of our financial system. And perhaps many years from now, you will regale your children and grandchildren with stories of how you lived through the Great Recession.